Saved but Stuck

For Every Believer Who is Tired of Pretending

SAVED BUT STUCK
For Every Believer Who Is Tired of Pretending

ISBN: 9798284313565
Copyright © 2025 by Rev. Anthony Miller
All rights reserved.

Scripture quotations are from The Holy Bible, English Standard Version® (ESV®), copyright © 2001 by Crossway, a publishing ministry of Good News Publishers. Used by permission. All rights reserved.

For anyone who has left Sunday's altar hot as fire, and woke up Monday cold as ice.

For anyone who has felt broken because they didn't get to feel "put back together".

For anyone who has ever been saved… but stuck.

Dear Reader,

If you're holding this book, I don't think it's by accident. I believe the Spirit of God is drawing you closer to Him right now, right in the middle of whatever mess, numbness, exhaustion, or quiet desperation you may be carrying.

For the duration of this book, we are friends. This is important because as I walked this road, I didn't feel like I had one. At least, not one I could *fully* trust, one who was *actually* there, one who supported me how I *needed* it. So throughout this book, as we walk forward together, I'll address you as such. I hope you don't mind… *friend.*

You need to know this book was not written from a place of perfection, but from the trenches. I've had late nights with an open Bible and a broken heart. I've prayed whispers through tears. I've been angry. I've wrestled with the same questions you might be asking:

> *"Why do I still feel stuck?"*
> *"Why can't I seem to change?"*
> *"Why does everyone else seem free but me?"*

If you've ever sat in a church and wondered why the worship didn't seem to reach you... If you've ever scrolled through Scripture but felt numb inside... If you've ever raised your hands while silently drowning in guilt, telling yourself to *"just get over it"*, or to *"ignore it"*... If you've ever loved Jesus but still felt stuck...

This book is for you.

Not the Sunday-morning you. Not the highlight-reel you. The real you. The one God sees when the lights are off and the performance ends.

In these pages, you won't find shame, you'll find honesty and grace from a friend who has walked this path and came out stronger when it was over. Maybe better yet, you'll find permission to **name what hurts** and faith to believe that healing is still possible.

Because the truth is: you can be saved, Spirit-filled, and still silently stuck. But friend, you don't have to stay there.

Jesus really does still breaks chains. He really does still walks through wildernesses. He really does still restore what religion and tradition of men have thrown away. Most importantly, He is still really calling you - not to impress Him, but to walk with Him. Not to fake it, but to follow Him into something real.

I can hear it now—in your mind, you're saying, "I've heard this before." It's hard to trust that this book, when you've been handed countless others, is really going to be any different. I know that because I've been where you are. I can speak to the Saved But Stuck Cycle, not because I've coined it in this book, but because I myself have gone round-and-round way too many times to count. With each spin, I tried:

- Praying about it
- Fasting about it
- Praying harder about it
- Fasting longer about it

And a million other "techniques" that didn't change me. Of course we need prayer and fasting, but what else? One time a woman went to her pastor's wife and admitted she was being physically abused. Upon hearing this, she said, "We'll be praying for you."

While she appreciated the prayers, she was already praying. She needed a strategy, accountability, and physical help to exit the situation.

Similarly, there have been several men who have been higher in stature than I come up to me and tell me they'd be my friend, my mentor, my stand-in father (after my father passed away), and many other titles. While I believe they were all well-meaning and well-intentioned, a title isn't enough. Though I was in desperate need of real help, I never received it.

This book is a result of figuring it out just between me and the Lord. Since I've figured it out, I've become the Lead Pastor of Hope Church of Iron Mountain, Michigan, and I've used these same strategies in leading that phenomenal congregation, as well as friends, family, co-workers, community members, and anyone else who has needed help along the way. In fact, I'm also a Social Work candidate at my local college, so this brings another layer of strength to this process.

The scientist, political commentator, and author, Ayesha Siddiqi, once said, "Be who you needed when you were younger." My Friend, that's exactly what I'm doing here in this book. And it's all for you.

So come as you are. Come with the relapse. With the regret. With the questions. With the frustration. With the rawness of a well-intentioned life that can't seem to find the salve. Come with the broken pieces. Come with all the almosts.

Bring it all, my Friend, and let's walk together toward the kind of freedom that lasts. You might be stuck right now, but you are not stuck forever.

With all my heart,

Your Friend,

Anthony

Pastor of the amazing Hope Church of Iron Mountain, Michigan, and recovering "Saved but Stuck" Christian

Foreword

There's a kind of weariness that not everyone talks about. Not the tired that comes from doing too much, but the kind that creeps in when you've done everything you know to do, and yet… still feel stuck.

I've been there.

I was pastoring a growing church, working a full-time job with overtime, and leading a ministry that impacted pastors across our state. Things looked fruitful. But inside? I was running on fumes. I had started to withdraw from my wife, my child, even my closest friends. I didn't know how to name what I was feeling, but I knew it wasn't good. Discouragement. Shame. The haunting sense that I was failing at something I couldn't quite fix.

One day, standing in our kitchen, my wife came up behind me and wrapped her arms around me. She just began to pray. I wanted to pull away. I did pull away. But she held on. And as she prayed, something in me broke open… and the Spirit of God began to lift that heavy fog. I'm telling you, it felt like someone had just saved my life.

From that moment, God began teaching me. Showing me how to abide in Him again. How to cast my cares instead of carrying them. How to live with Him, not just for Him.

That's why this book matters. That's why you're holding it in your hands.

Anthony Miller has lived what he writes. He's a man of integrity, passion, and perseverance. I've known him for about 20 years. Today, I'm honored to be his pastor. My wife and I have walked with him and his wife through disappointments that would've sidelined lesser men. But they kept showing up. Kept trusting. Kept serving.

This book is not a manual, it's a mirror. And it's honest. The chapter Don't Waste the Wilderness in particular spoke to me me because it resonated with a chord the Lord struck years ago. Though the wilderness can feel like an empty place, it's truly packed with the potential of a changed life… and Jesus is there with you if you reach for Him.

Anthony doesn't gloss over the moments we wish weren't part of the journey. He just brings them into the light, where healing can happen.

If you've ever felt like there must be more... like you love God but can't figure out why you're not growing the way you thought you would... If you've ever wondered if the stuck places are all there is... this book will speak to you. Not with hype. But with hope.

You're not alone, and you're not done.

Read this book slowly, pray through it, and let God meet you again.

Jay Jones
Servant, Pastor, Coach
Author of *The Habit Blueprint*

Table of Contents

Chapter 1: The Chains We Don't See   17
How bondage quietly becomes your normal.

Chapter 2: When Change Feels Impossible   41
Why grace matters in the struggle.

Chapter 3: God Wants to Walk With You   55
Closeness with God over performance.

Chapter 4: Fighting the Right Battle   71
Recognizing spiritual war and resisting well.

Chapter 5: The Power of Confession   89
Healing begins where hiding ends.

Chapter 6: Don't Waste the Wilderness   105
God forms you in dry seasons

Chapter 7: Learning to Live Free   121
Freedom is a lifestyle of abiding.

Conclusion: Our Table Talk   133
You are free, so walk like it.

Epilogue: The Journey Continues   141

Chapter One
The Chains We Don't See
Romans 7:18–25, Romans 8:1–2

The Lie That Feels Like Truth

Bondage is rarely chosen outright. Nobody rises in the morning and says, *"I think I'll be stuck today."* It creeps in, typically undetected, dressed like comfort, carrying the scent of survival. It masquerades as control while wrapping its arms around your soul like a cold chain. Before long, you stop noticing how heavy it is. You just learn to function in it.

Just ask Esau.

He didn't plan to trade his birthright that day. He didn't wake up planning to forfeit his future. He was just hungry. Tired. Empty. Vulnerable. And in that moment of exhaustion, what should've been unthinkable became... *negotiable.*

Jacob, ever the opportunist, offered him a bowl of stew. Something hot and immediate. Something easy. And Esau, desperate for relief, said yes. Sound familiar?

One bowl. One moment. One decision to satisfy a temporary craving. One decision cost him a blessing he could never get back.

My friend, that's how bondage often begins. Not with rebellion, but with relief. Not with a declaration, but a slow erosion. I know you're not trying to wreck your future. I believe you that you're not meaning to mess up. You're just trying to survive today.

Hear me clearly, though: survival decisions made without spiritual clarity will bankrupt your future in slow motion. Esau gave up something eternal for something easy. We have done the same.

We traded intimacy for attention.
We traded peace for control.
We traded purpose for applause.
We traded prayer for performance.
We traded faithfulness for attention spans.

And somewhere along the way, we got good at faking freedom. It just… happened.

We traded slow mornings with God for scrolling our phones. We traded stillness for busyness. We traded conviction for comfort and called it discipline. And all the while, something sacred was slipping through our very fingers. And while we were congratulating ourselves for keeping it all together, we were leaking spiritual vitality drop by drop. But here's the sinister part: we didn't even notice.

The enemy doesn't just throw chains at you - you'd notice that. Instead, he slips a veil over your eyes. Gradually and strategically. Layer by layer. Until dysfunction feels like normal, and confusion masquerades as clarity.

Paul said it like this: *"The god of this world has blinded the minds of the unbelievers"* (2 Corinthians 4:4). And while you may believe in God, that veil can still creep back in when survival becomes louder than surrender.

That's the real danger of The Hustle. We convince ourselves we're just holding it together. And that's the issue: **we** are holding **ourselves** together. What's worse is that we're doing it blind and without God. And by the time we realize what it's costing us, it's weeks, months, even years later… and we're stuck.

We didn't mean to. But like Esau, we were empty. We were tired. We were emotionally depleted. Our enemy is cunning; he doesn't make you an offer when you're strong, but waits until you're starving. Why? Because when you're starving, stew looks sacred.

And so the pattern begins. We settle for short-term comfort, and slowly, silently, we get stuck in cycles, mindsets, and in decisions we swore we'd never make. Then we wonder how we got here.

Esau didn't just lose a meal but he lost his identity. His legacy. He walked away with a full stomach, but an empty destiny. Friend, that's the danger of bondage: it disguises itself as relief.

But relief without repentance is a trap. And temporary satisfaction will always leave you spiritually malnourished.

You can't renounce what you won't recognize. You can't repent and continue to excuse. So before we go any further, ask yourself: What have I traded? Where did I settle? What seemed small in the moment but ended up costing me peace, clarity, or identity?

If you can name that, if you can recognize where the stew was offered, you can begin the journey back to wholeness. And I believe you can.

This is more than a moment. It becomes a pattern. And the longer you stay in survival mode, the more it feels spiritual. That's what I call a faith relapse. You believe, but barely. You show up, but you shut down. You quote the promises, but stop expecting them to be true for you.

You want to believe, but you feel too numb. You try to grow, but default to what's familiar. You have just enough church to keep up appearances, but not enough presence to change.

It happens quietly.

You learn how to laugh while feeling spiritually numb. You learn how to serve in church while privately addicted to something you swore you'd quit. You learn how to shout in worship while scrolling through filth alone later. That's not freedom - that's survival. The trap of survival mode is it teaches you how to function in captivity.

You start mistaking numbness for peace. Silence for healing. Busyness for breakthrough. You stop expecting joy. Stop fighting for clarity. Stop praying with fire. And the worst part? You get good at being stuck.

We've learned how to smile while slowly suffocating. We've crafted spiritual posts while quietly ignoring what God is whispering in our private moments. We've shouted in services while hiding compromise in silence.

And so, we renamed bondage. We justified dysfunction. We wore chains and called them quirks. And over time, the veil slips back over our eyes.

But it doesn't stop there. The enemy doesn't just shackle your hands, he clouds your vision. He keeps you busy enough to ignore the damage, blind enough to keep stumbling, numb enough to believe you're fine. See, he doesn't need to make you evil. He just needs you to settle. Settled Christians don't scare hell. Settled Christians are only a threat to themselves.

Here's the truth: you can't fix what you refuse to face, and you can't truly face what you're continuing to rename and normalize. So let's pause right here. What's holding you? What's hiding behind *"I'm fine"* and *"God knows my heart"*? What have you tolerated because it was easier than confronting it?

Because if it's holding you, and God didn't give it to you, it's bondage.

Jesus didn't endure the cross so you could adjust your chains. He went there to break them. Jesus didn't die for half-freedom. He came to set the captives free. Not moderately managed, not slightly improved. Free.

I dare you to believe that numb isn't normal.

But Anthony, I've Gotten Good at Being Stuck.
I know that, because I was just as good at it. We know how to smile in public while sinking in private. We know how to post something spiritual online while ignoring what God is whispering to us in prayer. We know how to shout in church and scroll through filth alone later. We know how to say, "God is good," even when our hearts feel hollow.

That's not freedom, it's survival. That's functioning in captivity. The problem with surviving in bondage is that you start treating abnormal as normal. You start believing that peace is for other people. That joy is for the spiritually elite. That freedom is real... but not for you. And that's exactly how the enemy wants it.

James 1:14–15: *"But each person is tempted when he is lured and enticed by his own desire. Then desire when it has conceived gives birth to sin, and sin when it is fully grown brings forth death."*

Friend, did you catch that? This doesn't happen all at once. It starts with desire. Then comes deception. Then comes sin. And then, eventually, death. Not always physical death. But death of joy, of purpose, of hope, of identity. That's what happens when we get good at being stuck.

We get so comfortable managing symptoms that we don't even realize the sickness has spread. We don't notice how far we've drifted because we're still *"doing the right things."* But inside, something is shutting down. The voice of conviction gets quieter. The appetite for the presence of God weakens. Over time, what used to grieve us no longer stirs us at all.

So you settle. You stop fighting. You stop hoping. You stop asking for more. You just go through the motions. Stuck but bound, breathing but stuck. But hear me: That is not the life Jesus died for you to live. He didn't go to the cross just so you could cope better. He came to set captives free! Not manageably restrained, not semi-okay, but free.

The Secret Struggle Most People Never See

Most chains aren't visible, and that's why they're so dangerous. You can be in leadership and be bound. You can be married and be bound. You can tithe, serve, and sing on Sunday, and still cry yourself to sleep, convinced you'll never change.

Some chains come from trauma. Some from pride. Some from survival strategies we picked up as kids that became strongholds in adulthood. Others are born in places of pain where we were never taught how to grieve properly, forgive fully, or surrender consistently.

For example: Bitterness is a chain that starts out as a defense mechanism. "I'll never let anyone hurt me like that again."

Perfectionism is a chain that comes from a wound. "If I can just do everything right, maybe I'll be accepted."

Addiction is often not about pleasure, it's about numbing pain.

Control issues are not always about ego. Sometimes they're about fear.

Lust isn't always about lust. Sometimes it's about loneliness and worth.

Overcommitment isn't always about purpose, sometimes it's about not wanting to face what we'd feel in stillness.

Your stuck place has a story. But just because it has a story doesn't mean it gets to write your future. If you're exhausted from trying to be a 'good Christian' while still feeling like a prisoner to your own patterns, Paul gets it.

More importantly, God has already made a way out.

Paul Knew the Battle Too

Paul, the apostle who planted churches, raised the dead, and penned most of the New Testament, describes in Romans 7 a brutal kind of inner conflict:

"For I have the desire to do what is right, but not the ability to carry it out. For I do not do the good I want, but the evil I do not want is what I keep on doing."

You've been there. You've cried out at an altar, "God, I'll never do it again," only to fall again by Friday night. You've made promises to your spouse or yourself or your pastor or your prayer journal, and meant every word of them, only to feel like a hypocrite the next week.

You're not alone. You're not strange. You're not disqualified. You're just human. And this battle? It's real.

It's not just a moment of weakness; it's a spiritual law, Paul says. *"When I want to do right, evil lies close at hand."* There's a war in your members. A tug-of-war between what your spirit longs for and what your flesh still craves. Between who you are in Christ and who you used to be without Him.

This is not an excuse. But it is an explanation. It's not a license to live bound, but it is a roadmap to understand what's going on. Paul isn't glorifying struggle. He's exposing it. He's saying, "I know what it's like to love Jesus and still feel trapped."

If you've ever felt the same, welcome to the club. And welcome to the turning point.

Wretched but Not Worthless

The chapter climaxes in a cry: *"Wretched man that I am! Who will deliver me from this body of death?"*

That word wretched sounds harsh. It doesn't fit the curated Instagram version of Paul. But he says it anyway. Because he's not dressing it up. He's not pretending. He's crying out in holy frustration.

Maybe you've been there too. Crying in your car. Clenching your fists in your bedroom. Whispering into the night, *"God, why can't I just be free?"*

What's beautiful is that Paul doesn't stay in despair. He doesn't wallow in it. He shifts. He pivots. He lifts his eyes.

"Thanks be to God through Jesus Christ our Lord!"

He goes from "wretched" to worship. From frustration to freedom. From agony to awareness that deliverance does not come from trying harder, but from surrendering deeper.

And that's when the real breakthrough happens.

There Is Now No Condemnation

The very next verse, Romans 8:1, is one of the most liberating sentences in Scripture: *"There is therefore now no condemnation for those who are in Christ Jesus."*

Not later. Not when you get it all together. Not when you've proven yourself for six months. Now. Right now.

Right in the middle of your cycle. Right in the middle of your relapse. Right in the middle of your battle. No condemnation. Not because God's standards have changed, but because Jesus paid the full price. This isn't a pass for sin. This is power over it. Because grace doesn't give you a license to stay bound.

Grace gives you the key to walk out of the prison.

The Law of the Spirit

Romans 8:2 adds this thunderbolt: *"For the law of the Spirit of life has set you free in Christ Jesus from the law of sin and death."*

This means there's a new law in effect. A higher law. Like the law of aerodynamics overcomes the law of gravity, the Spirit's power overcomes sin's pull.

That doesn't mean you won't feel the pull anymore. But it does mean you no longer have to obey it.

You're not powerless. You're not stuck. The chains might be familiar, but they are not permanent.

What Freedom Requires

Freedom isn't just about a church service or a spiritual high. It's about surrendering to the process. Freedom will cost you:

Your pride.
You've got to be willing to admit you need help.

Your comfort.
You'll have to disrupt routines that have kept you spiritually numb.

Your hiding.
You'll need to walk in the light, even when it feels vulnerable.

The price is worth it, because the cost of staying bound is far higher than the cost of getting free. And you don't have to do it alone.

That's why God places us in community, called "The Body of Christ." He places us in relationships where we can be honest, accountable, encouraged, and reminded of the truth when we forget.

You Are Not What Bound You
You are not your mistake. You are not your addiction. You are not your lowest moment. You are not the version of yourself that hurt people. You are not the sin that held you. You are not what they did to you. You are not what you did to yourself.

You are His. And in Him, you are no longer stuck.

Let's get practical. How do you start to break free from something that's held you so long?

Name It Clearly
You can't break a chain you refuse to admit is there.

Stop using language that makes bondage sound cute:

"I've just got a temper."
Or, is it unresolved rage tied to rejection?

"It's just how I am."
Or, is it trauma you've never healed from?

"I know I could be better."
Or, *"I'm bound and don't know how to change?"*

Write it down. Say it out loud, and bring it into the light.

Track the Pattern
Most strongholds operate like cycles. You fall. You feel shame. You try to fix it. You burn out. You fall again. Pay attention to:

When you're most vulnerable (time of day, mood, isolation, stress).

What triggers you (rejection, anxiety, conflict, fatigue).

How you cope (distraction, overworking, escaping, sin).

Awareness is not freedom, but it's the first doorway to it.

Interrupt the Cycle

You don't have to fix your whole life in one moment, but you can interrupt the cycle. Here's a simple phrase to try: "This time, I'm not going to hide. I'm going to pray and reach out instead."

You can text someone. You can stop scrolling. You can get on your knees. You can go outside. You can change the playlist. You can do something different in the moment, and that moment becomes holy ground.

Community Is the Context of Freedom

Most people stay bound because they refuse to get honest with someone else.

Yes, Jesus is enough. But Jesus gave us His Body for a reason. You were never meant to heal alone. Freedom requires a safe space to confess, process, and grow. Find a mentor. Find a prayer partner. Join a life group. Reach out to a trusted pastor. Doing these things will create rhythms where light can regularly hit your dark places. Confession breaks the silence. Accountability breaks the cycle.

When couples ask us to do marriage counseling with them, we've found that sometimes, one spouse is very reluctant and wants the other one to go by themselves. This is an example of Accountability Aversion—the tendency to protect oneself from negative consequences, or, the tendency to avoid taking responsibility for one's actions. See, there are always three sides to every story: your side, their side, and the truth. Accountability helps you see the two sides that you'd prefer to ignore.

What to Do Now
1. Name the Chains.
Write down the top three areas where you feel stuck. Don't dress them up. Don't spiritualize them. Call them what they are: addiction, fear, insecurity, comparison, compromise, apathy. Freedom begins with truth.

2. Invite God into the Real Room.
Bring those areas into your next prayer time. Say it plainly. "God, I'm stuck here and I don't want to be." Don't perform or plead. Just surrender.

3. Confess to Someone Who Can Handle the Truth.
Pick one trusted, spiritually grounded person who is mature in grace and truth. Share what's been holding you. Let them pray over you.

4. Create a Chain Disruption Plan.
What triggers you? What environment, time of day, or thought pattern feeds the cycle? Don't wait to feel strong, proactively plan for the moment you feel weak. Set boundaries. Choose pre-decisions. Build a way out.

5. Speak the Truth Every Morning.
Post Romans 8:1 where you'll see it like on a mirror, phone lock screen, fridge. Declare it daily: *"There is therefore now no condemnation for those who are in Christ Jesus."* Say it until it sounds true. Say it until the chain starts to shake.

Before You Turn The Page

There's still time for you. There's still hope for you. There's still a way forward. Chains may be familiar, but they are not final. You don't have to stay where you are. This is your Exodus. This is your moment. This is where the cycle ends—and freedom begins.

Reflection Questions

What are the chains in your life that you've grown comfortable with?

In what ways have you been managing rather than confronting them?

Who do you need to bring into the journey with you?

How does knowing "there is now no condemnation" shift how you see your struggle?

What's one small, tangible step you can take today toward freedom?

Scriptures to Read and Meditate On
Romans 7:18–25
Romans 8:1–2
2 Corinthians 10:4–5
Psalm 32:5
Galatians 5:1
James 5:16
John 8:36

Prayer
Lord, I've been stuck. And if I'm honest, I've made peace with some of my chains. But today I'm choosing honesty over hiding. I want freedom more than I want comfort. Help me name what's binding me. Help me surrender it instead of managing it. Thank You for grace that meets me in the middle of my mess. Thank You for freedom that's already been won. Walk me out of this prison, one step at a time. I believe freedom is for me. In Jesus' name, Amen.

Chapter Two
When Change Feels Impossible
Romans 7:21–25, Romans 8:3–4,
2 Corinthians 12:7–10

This chapter is for the person who's tired of the cycle.

You started strong, you had your moment of deliverance, and you felt lighter. You prayed, fasted, and filled pages of a journal with hope. Maybe you even got baptized, rededicated your life, or were filled with the Holy Spirit. And for a while, you really believed it was over. The old thing, the dark thing, the heavy thing—it felt finished.

But then something happened. The urge returned. The old mindset crept back in. The people you distanced yourself from started "randomly" showing up again. And little by little, you slipped. Again. You thought, "Was I ever really changed? I guess not."

But you don't feel bound in the same way as before. You know the truth, but you're still getting stuck in fear, old habits, pride, anxiety, comparison, isolation. Maybe you picked up a bottle on the way home, *"just in case."* Let's call it what it is, even if it stings: You're saved, but stuck. And God didn't save you to stay that way.

The Internal War
Paul describes it like this: *"So I find it to be a law that when I want to do right, evil lies close at hand."*

Have you ever gotten to a point in your spiritual journey where you felt like you were chasing your tail? Like your prayer life is inconsistent despite best efforts, your mind is noisy though you tell yourself to be quiet, your desires are divided in spite of knowing the end result, and your strength is just... gone? I've been there so many times. Too many times.

Maybe you get up early, determined to pray, but end up falling asleep on your knees. You delete that app, cut the ties, make the vow, and still somehow end up back where you swore you wouldn't go. After all, you can manage, right? At church you raise your hands and sing the song but feel like you're just going through the motions while silently wondering why you're still not free. Maybe you lay in bed at night replaying every failure. Wishing you could rewind the conversation, regretting the moment of weakness and grieving the person you want to be, but aren't yet.

Deep down, you're scared that this is it. That this version of you is the only version that will ever exist. That God has run out of patience. That you're just not strong enough. That being stuck is just your lot in life.

If that's you, like it was me, I want you to know that you are not crazy. You are not weak. And no, you are not a fake.

You are experiencing what I call *The Tension of Transformation*. Just like when a broken bone starts to heal, it often hurts more before it gets stronger. That tension between pain and healing is where many believers get discouraged because they assume that once they decide to change, things should get easier. I admit, I still think it "should"! But the truth is, sometimes it gets harder first. I hope you find strength in simply reading this admission— sometimes it really does get *harder*.

It's not harder because change isn't happening, but because of this truth: your enemy doesn't fight what doesn't threaten him.

And often, the deeper the surrender, the louder the resistance. The closer you get to breakthrough, the more the enemy whispers, *"You're just going to give it up again. This is who you are. The failure. The Wheel-Spinner. You haven't really changed. It's the same as it always was. You'll always be this way."*

Friend, these are lies. But I have to warn you: if you don't learn to identify the lies, you'll wear them like truth.

Grace Is Not Fragile

Let's make one thing clear: struggling doesn't disqualify you. It doesn't mean God has left you, written you off, or filed you under "too much."

God's grace is not fragile. It doesn't break when you fall. It doesn't thin out when you mess up. It isn't handed to you with a sigh and a side-eye. Grace is not for the polished, it is for those who push forward even though they're not. It is the force that lifts you when you don't even want to get out of bed. Scripture proves this over and over.

Titus 2:11-12 says, *"For the grace of God has appeared, bringing salvation for all people, training us to renounce ungodliness and worldly passions,* and to live self-controlled, upright, and godly lives in the present age." Let that sink in.

Grace doesn't just clean up your past but it steps into your present and walks with you toward your future. It exists to disciple you. The grace of God is there to coach you, to teach you, to walk with you. It's not just the eraser for your failures; it's the trainer for your future.

So if you're struggling, if you're tempted, if you're face-down in shame, remember this: grace isn't just at the end of your mess waiting to congratulate you for crawling out of it. It climbs into the ditch, cups your face, and says, "We're getting out of here."

Hebrews 4:16 declares, "Let us then with confidence draw near to the throne of grace, that we may receive mercy and find grace to help in time of need."

Romans 5:20 reminds us that, "Where sin increased, grace abounded all the more..." God is not outpaced by your issues. You cannot out-sin, out-wear, or out-stumble His grace.

Paul, the man who wrote those very verses, once begged God to take his thorn away. But God didn't remove it. Instead, He gave Paul something better: *"My grace is sufficient for you, for my power is made perfect in weakness."*

Maybe you've been asking God to take something away: The temptation, the insecurity, the depression, the fear, the addiction.

But instead of just plucking it out of your life the easy way, maybe God is telling you what He told Paul: I'm giving you grace instead. Grace that empowers. Grace to keep showing up. Grace to say no when everything in you wants to say yes. Grace to love when it hurts. Grace to hold your peace. Grace to keep going when progress feels slow.

Not because you're strong. But because grace is.

Before You Give Up

I know what it's like to ache for change. To cry out in the dark wondering why you can't seem to get free. To beg God through tears, only to fall again. To walk into church with hands lifted and a heavy heart. To feel like you're drowning in silence while everyone else seems to be floating in victory.

I've been the one who preached faith while battling fear. I've prayed for others to be delivered while secretly wishing someone would do the same for me. I've laid hands on others and walked away wondering, "But who's going to help *me*?"

I've looked in the mirror and hated who I saw. Not because I didn't believe in grace, but because I didn't think it applied to someone like me. I let my failures define me. I believed the lie that *what I did* was *who I was*. I've called myself, like Paul, the Chief of Sinners, a liar, an adulterer, a scam artist, a clown, a luster, a jerk, a terrible human being, and many others, most of them being much worse and more colorful.

But hear me: You are not too far gone. You are not disqualified. You are not too weak. You are not alone.

I don't care how many times you've fallen, and I don't care how long it's been. I don't care what you did last night. If you're still reaching, if you're still praying, if you're still hoping or even breathing at all... God is not done with you.

Galatians 6:9 says, *"Let us not grow weary of doing*

good, for in due season we will reap, if we do not give up."

That's our key right there: If you do not give up.

Not if you're perfect. Not if you never mess up again. Just... **if you don't quit.**

Don't you dare give up, Friend. Don't stop showing up. Don't silence your praise. Don't skip the altar call. Don't retreat back into shame and pretend like grace ran out—like you used up all He had.

You are not stuck because God abandoned you. You're stuck because your flesh has been louder than His Spirit. But He's calling again. Right now. In the middle of your battle. In the middle of your relapse. In the middle of your questions.

He is not angry. He is not pacing. He is not surprised. He is reaching. If you take even one step, He will meet you with mercy. If you whisper even one word, He will flood you with grace. If you lift your eyes, He will lift your life. So get up. Cry if you must, crawl if you have to, but move forward.

Keep walking.

Keep repenting.
Keep surrendering.
Keep praying.
Keep going.

This is not your ending. It's your turning point.

What to Do Now
1. Start with a 7-Day Surrender Rhythm
Every morning this week, before the noise rushes in, begin with this simple prayer: *"Lord, this day is Yours. My strength is not enough, but Your Spirit is. Lead me, help me, hold me steady."* Say it before scrolling, before the tasks, before the voices. Let surrender be your starting point.

2. Name the Chain
What's been holding you? Don't list everything. Choose one area where you feel most stuck, like shame, anger, lust, fear, isolation, performance, and bring it into the light. Write it down. Pray over it. Ask God to show you what's beneath it. Then tell one person you trust.

3. Prepare for the Next Battle
Freedom doesn't just come from intention, but preparation. What will you do the next time that trigger hits or temptation knocks? Who will you text? Where will you go? What Scripture will you speak? Don't just resist. Get ready. Build a battle plan.

4. Return to the Basics
This week, commit to four simple rhythms:

10 minutes in the Word
10 minutes in prayer
1 intentional act of obedience (big or small)
1 moment of written gratitude

You're not trying to earn anything. You're building muscle. Start small, stay consistent. For more on healthy and Biblical habits, see *The Habit Blueprint* by Rev. Jay Jones.

5. Reach for a Person of Grace
You weren't meant to do this alone. Text someone who knows how to love and speak truth. Say, "I don't want to stay stuck. Can I walk this out with you?" Let them in. Let them walk with you.

Before You Turn The Page

You may still feel stuck, but *stuck* is not your identity. Stuck is not rebellion. Stuck is not rejection. Stuck is the tension before transformation. So don't wait for the feeling to change before you move. Take a step. Say the prayer and speak the truth. Reach for help. Freedom is not a future reward for flawless behavior. It's a present invitation for honest surrender. Start now. Not when you're stronger or when you're certain. Right here, in your wrestle. Because Jesus meets you in motion and His grace walks with you the whole way.

Reflection Questions

What are the clearest signs that you're stuck right now?

What emotional, relational, or spiritual patterns seem to pull you back the most?

In what ways have you misunderstood or misused grace in your journey?

Who in your life can walk with you and hold you accountable?

Scriptures to Read and Meditate On
Romans 7:21–25
Romans 8:3–4
2 Corinthians 12:7–10
James 5:16
Titus 2:11–12
Galatians 6:9
Hebrews 4:16
Isaiah 43:18–19
Philippians 2:13

Prayer
Lord, I bring You the parts of me that feel stuck. The parts that feel heavy, that wrestle, that war. You know the cycles. You see the struggle. But You also see what I can't yet see: healing, wholeness, and breakthrough. I choose surrender over striving. I say yes to grace instead of guilt. Teach me to walk by Your Spirit. Give me strength to keep showing up. Help me unlearn the lies, embrace Your truth, and trust You in the middle. I declare I am not finished, I am not forgotten, and I am not bound to who I used to be. In Jesus' name, Amen.

Chapter Three
God Wants to Walk With You
Genesis 3:8-10, Micah 6:8, John 14:16-17
Galatians 5:16-25

There's something deep in the heart of God that has always longed for closeness with His people.

Closeness.

From the beginning, God didn't just want people who would behave. He wanted sons and daughters who would walk with Him. That was the design: Intimacy. Relationship. Life with Him, not just obedience to Him. In Genesis 3, before sin ever fractured the world, God came walking in the garden in the cool of the day. That wasn't a one-time event. It was a rhythm. A routine. A relationship.

But then Adam and Eve sinned. They ran. They hid. They covered themselves in fig leaves, full of fear and shame. And what does God do?

He shows up.

Then He asks one of the most powerful questions in all of Scripture: *"Where are you?"*

He didn't say, *"How could you?"*
He didn't say, *"What have you done?"*
He didn't thunder from the heavens with a lecture.

Nope. He asked a question. A gentle, Father-hearted, soul-searching question. **Where are you?**

That wasn't about GPS location. That was about spiritual posture. Hear me: God knew where Adam's body was, but He was asking Adam to recognize where his heart had gone.

This is the beauty of grace: even when we hide, God still seeks. Even when shame makes us cover up and run, He still shows up to walk with us. His first recorded response to Adam and Eve's sin was not fury. It was invitation.

I believe that question is still echoing into your life today.

"Where are you?"

Not because He can't find you. He can. He already has. But He's giving you the chance to come out of hiding. To peel off the fig leaves. To step out from the shame. To be seen—truly seen—and to be loved.

Let that wreck you a little. Let it settle on you. The God of creation didn't storm away when you fell. He came closer.

This is not your moment to perform or to prove, but to respond to His question.

"Where are you?"

If you can answer that honestly and humbly, even if it's a whisper, then you're already on your way back into the walk He designed you for all along.

What Walking With God Actually Looks Like
Let's break a myth right now: walking with God doesn't mean living on a spiritual high 24/7/365. It doesn't mean you feel goosebumps every morning, or get prophetic dreams every night. It doesn't mean you always have the right words to say the most perfect prayers. *Thank goodness.*

Walking with God means you show up daily and honestly. It means including Him in your ordinary. Talking to Him in frustration. Letting Him speak into your day before you speak into someone else's. It means talking with Him when you're frustrated. Yes, you are allowed to share frustrations with God. You are even allowed to be frustrated with or by God. He has big, broad shoulders. He can take it.

Walking with God means:
- Letting Him speak into your schedule.
- Letting Him nudge you before you respond.
- Letting Him sit with you in silence when there are no words.

Galatians 5 says that if we walk by the Spirit, we will not gratify the desires of the flesh. In other words, the more I stay in-step with Him, the less I fall into the patterns that used to trap me.

I wish this came auto-magically, but it doesn't. It comes over time, through alignment. And alignment requires attention and intention.

The Fruit Follows the Flow

Paul doesn't say "try harder to love, be joyful, stay peaceful, be patient." He says "walk by the Spirit." Then the fruit of that walk shows in our lives.

Too many of us are exhausted trying to manufacture what only grows through connection. We strain to be fruitful, but we've cut off the flow. We're trying to grow fruit in a disconnected life.

We memorize Scriptures but ignore the Spirit. We sing songs but silence conviction. We perform spiritually but don't abide personally. We speak in tongues at church and cuss in the car on the way home.

And here's what happens: We go through the motions, playing the part. We know how to smile and say *"I'm blessed"* while secretly withering inside. We serve, preach, sing, volunteer. After all, *that's what we're supposed to do, right?* Ignore the problem and "pray it away"? The well is dry, and we know it.

Eventually, the weight of pretending wears you down. And when the fruit doesn't come, we blame the church, blame the pastor, blame the people around us, and we blame God.

We're *Church Hurt* ™.

"I tried everything and nothing changed."
"I did the right things and still feel empty."
"Why is it working for them and not for me?"

The truth is, Friend, fruit is not a performance. It's a byproduct. You don't get apples from effort, you get them from abiding. You don't produce peace by forcing yourself to chill out. Peace is the fruit of the Spirit, not the flesh. Joy isn't manufactured with fake smiles. It flows from connection.

John 15:4-5 says, *"Remain in Me, as I also remain in you. No branch can bear fruit by itself; it must remain in the vine. Neither can you bear fruit unless you remain in Me... apart from Me you can do nothing."*

You can preach a sermon and still be dry. You can go to Bible study and still lack fruit. You can know doctrine and still lack kindness, joy, gentleness, and self-control.

So ask yourself: Am I bearing fruit or faking fruit? Am I connected or just committed? Am I intimate with God or just involved with His stuff?

God is not asking you to *perform* fruitfulness. He's asking you to walk with Him.

And when you walk with Him, talk with Him, lean into Him, and surrender to Him, the fruit comes naturally. Not all at once. Not in perfect balance. But gradually, steadily, and authentically. Because where the Spirit flows, fruit will grow.

Psalm 1:3, *"He is like a tree planted by streams of water that yields its fruit in its season, and its leaf does not wither. In all that he does, he prospers."*

When the Walk Feels Dry

I'll be honest about this, because some people aren't: not every season of walking with God feels refreshing. There are dry seasons when your prayers feel hollow and the Word feels distant. Seasons when the routine feels heavier than usual. You do all the things on the Christianity Checklist. You read the Bible, show up to church, try to worship, but it just feels like nothing is breaking through.

It feels like showing up to a well and finding it dry. You keep drawing, hoping something will change. But inside, you're tired. Spiritually dehydrated and running on fumes.

It can feel like you're the only one. Like you're somehow broken. Like everyone else is hearing God's voice, having breakthroughs, getting goosebumps in worship, and you're just... there. Dry.

It can make you question your faith. *"Is something wrong with me? Did I do something to make God back away?"* It can even make you resent the joy you see in others. You're glad for them, but deep down you wonder, *"Why not me?"*

There are days it doesn't feel like you're *walking* with God. It feels like limping. Like crawling. Like dragging your lame feet while you pretend you're preparing for the marathon with the best of them. This is the part church folk love to skip. They sing about victory, shout about overflow, but rarely admit when it feels dry. Who talks about just trying to survive spiritually? About when your hands are lifted but your heart feels cold? About when the Scripture hits your eyes but not your spirit? About when you leave church frustrated instead of refreshed?

Here's what I want you to know: dry seasons happen to **everyone**. Yes, even *them*.

Every believer, even the most seasoned, even the most passionate, walks through spiritual dryness at some point. It doesn't mean you've lost your relationship with God. It doesn't mean you've failed. It just means you're human.

Not too long ago, someone I had been mentoring sent me this message about dryness:

"I had to deal with it again—the distance, the dryness. I felt as if I was doing something wrong, or maybe it was that I wasn't doing enough. But all He wanted was more of me. Sometimes we feel like He is not near us, or has been distant from us when we need Him most. But just know that He never will never let us down. There is light at the end of this dark tunnel you're in right now. Maybe you're getting too comfortable where you are right now, and He is wanting more of you, too. Maybe He wants you to draw closer to Himself, and so that is why you're not feeling that same connection you felt in the very beginning. You are still His child, and you are on the best path you can ever be in. Keep seeking His face."

God is still near and His Spirit still speaks. And often, your roots are growing deeper even though you don't feel like they're growing at all. I have learned that some of the greatest growth happens when you feel the least.

Isaiah 58:11 says, *"The Lord will guide you continually and satisfy your desire in scorched places and make your bones strong; and you shall be like a watered garden, like a spring of water, whose waters do not fail."*

Even in a scorched place, the Spirit can sustain you. In dry seasons, it's not about feeling your way through. It's about faithfully showing up. That's why Micah 6:8 says, *"What does the Lord require of you but to do justice, and to love kindness, and to walk humbly with your God?"* Not sprint. Not impress. Not float in spiritual ecstasy. Just walk. One step at a time. Dry or not, He's walking with you still.

The big names in our denominal organizations aren't any more loved than you, and they don't have any special access card that gets them closer to Jesus. He is no respecter of persons. The difference? They show up every day. Do you?

What to Do Now

1. Begin Each Day With Intentional Welcome
Start your mornings with this prayer: "Holy Spirit, I welcome You today. Help me to stay in step with You."

2. Identify a Distraction or Divider
What consistently pulls your attention away from God's presence? What dulls your sensitivity? Limit or lay it down this week.

3. Add One Daily Moment of Stillness
Take five minutes each day to sit in silence. No phone. No background noise. Just a posture of listening. Write down anything God impresses on your heart.

4. Practice the "Ask First" Habit
Before responding to stress, making a decision, or giving your opinion—pause and ask, "Holy Spirit, what are You saying?"

5. Notice the Fruit
At the end of each day, reflect: Where did I respond with love, patience, or gentleness today? Celebrate those moments. That's fruit.

What to Do Now

1. Begin the Day with Anticipation Welcome Start each morning with this prayer: "Holy Spirit, I welcome you. Guide, help me today in everything I do."

2. Identify a Distraction or Burden What consistently pulls your attention away from God's presence? What do you spend energy on? Jot it down this week.

3. Ask God in the Moment to Step In When you notice your worry rising, in silence or out loud, pause and more than a just react. In that silence, invite anything God has assigned to you most ...

4. Form the Ask-First Habit Before responding to an email, picture a decision, or before you come phone and ask, "Holy Spirit, what are you seeing?"

5. Record the Results At the end of each day, reflect: "Where did I respond today?" Write down one or two specific changes God made, Identify to share one with someone.

66

Before You Turn The Page

You were never meant to do this alone. God's Holy Spirit is not a concept. He is a Companion. You are not stuck trying to behave your way into God's favor. You are being invited to walk. So walk, because He's already walking toward you. Not because you have it all together. I believe in you.

Reflection Questions

1. What does walking with God look like in your real, daily life?

2. Where are you most often out of step with the Spirit?

3. How do you usually respond when your walk feels dry?

4. What is one change you can make this week to walk more closely with God?

Scriptures to Read and Meditate On
Genesis 3:8-10
Micah 6:8
Galatians 5:16-25
John 14:16-17
Romans 8:5-6
Psalm 63:1-8

Prayer
Lord, I want to walk with You. I don't want to run ahead or fall behind. I want to stay close. Tune my heart to Your voice. Quiet the noise that pulls me away. Forgive me for trying to bear fruit without staying rooted. Teach me to abide. Teach me to listen. Teach me to yield. Thank You for walking with me in every season—even when I feel dry, even when I feel distant. I trust that You're near, and I choose to follow, step by step. In Jesus' name, Amen.

Chapter Four
Fighting the Right Battle
Ephesians 6:10–18, 2 Corinthians 10:3–5,
Romans 8:5–6, 1 Peter 5:8–10

Many of the most defeated people I know are not lazy. They're not rebellious, and it's not even that they're faithless. They're just fighting the wrong battles. They're tired because they've been shadowboxing. They're anxious because they're constantly on edge. They're discouraged, not because they don't care, but because they do. Deeply. They want to do right. They want to grow. They want to move forward. But it feels like every time they take a step, something pushes back.

In the absence of clarity, they start swinging at symptoms instead of strongholds.

They fight their spouse instead of their bitterness. Their kids instead of their frustration. Their pastor instead of their inconsistencies. Their church instead of confronting their offense. Their own reflection, when their real enemy is their insecurity.

This shows up in the day-to-day stuff: The way your

heart races when a certain topic comes up. The way you isolate yourself after a conflict. The way you overreact to something small, because you haven't healed from something big. It shows up in the mental exhaustion, in the cycles you can't seem to break, in the quiet wondering:

Why is this still so hard?

Let me show you how this plays out... She came to church every Sunday, served faithfully on her team, raised her hands in worship, and conveniently had to use the restroom as soon as the altar call began. Every time. Not because she didn't want prayer, but because she didn't know how to admit the problem and name the heaviness. Her husband had shut down emotionally. Her job drained her. Her heart felt miles away from God. And all she could think was, *"If I just try harder, I'll get better. Life will get better."*

So she did. She volunteered more, she smiled wider, and doubled-down on manufactured joy. But inside she was losing it because she was trying to win a spiritual war with emotional effort.

She loved Jesus, but didn't trust in His love enough

to let Him help her. Unfortunately, I see this in too many Christians.

I know what it is to feel worn out, spiritually and emotionally, without even knowing why. To feel like you're doing all the right things, but still losing ground. I know what it feels like to check everything off that list and still feel like you're not good enough.

Sooner or later, you start to believe it's you. That you're what's broken. That you're the one that's too messed up, too emotional, too weak, too sensitive, too late, too far gone. What if your issue is that you're swinging at the wrong target?

Paul writes in Ephesians 6: *"For we do not wrestle against flesh and blood, but against the rulers... the authorities... the cosmic powers over this present darkness... the spiritual forces of evil in the heavenly places."*

This is not a metaphor for some far-away philosophy, he's writing here about the actual battle we all face, and if you don't recognize it, you'll keep losing no matter how hard you fight to win.

Friend, you can't cast out what you're busy cuddling. You can't rebuke what you're still entertaining. You can't win a war you won't admit exists. You can't win a spiritual war without being submitted to your ultimate spiritual leader—Jesus Christ.

The Battlefield of the Mind

If the enemy can influence your thoughts, he doesn't need to chain your wrists and ankles. I have learned over time that every spiritual stronghold has a mental doorway. That's why 2 Corinthians 10 tells us that our weapons are not carnal, but mighty through God to pull down strongholds and demolish arguments.

Your mind is where most of the battle is focused on, and therefore, we should start treating our mind like spiritual territory. Before we make financial, relational, or habit decisions that are antithetical to our Christian walk, roots develop in our thoughts.

Temptation begins as a suggestion: *"Just one time. No one has to know."*

Shame starts as a whisper: *"You're not really free. You never will be."*

Bitterness from a replayed moment: *"They should have known better. They never cared anyway."*

Your thoughts are not neutral. They are either aligned with Truth, or they are open to attack. I do not think some conservative religious folk were necessarily ill-meaning when they preached against having televisions in homes years ago. They understood the truth that the minds and the thought-lives of their parishioners were spiritual targets, and they recognized the evil associated with televisions. Unfortunately, in some cases, instead of discipling their congregations on how to protect their minds and make God-honoring decisions, they just taught that the TV was a devil-created evil and nobody should have one.

In Joshua 24, he is recorded to say that for him and his house, they will serve the Lord. If televisions were available in Joshua's time, would he have one? I hope you can see now the struggle associated with the mind, and how nuanced the issue can be. The human mind is sacred space where our theology becomes practice, where truth becomes identity, and where lies become strongholds.

When this happens, it feels like getting out of bed already tired, scrolling through social media and feeling like you're not enough. It feels like having one awkward conversation at church and obsessing over it for the next week.

It feels like laying your head on the pillow, exhausted, only to hear your mind scream with regret, insecurity, fear, or anger. But you don't tell anyone for shame.

It feels like knowing better but not doing better, and hating yourself for it.

This is the war we all fight. It's exhausting. Mental warfare can wear you out before you ever realize your real assignment, and that's why some people never build what God called them to build, because they're too tired from just surviving their own thoughts.

But hear me: struggling with your thoughts doesn't mean you're not saved. You can be saved, but stuck. If anything, the struggle is often proof that you are saved.

Before Christ, you didn't fight your thoughts, you just followed them. You agreed with your flesh and justified your sin. You lived in sin without resistance. You lied because others didn't deserve the truth. You withheld apologies or forgiveness because they did you wrong. You lusted because you needed relief from stress. I get it.

But now? We would do good to recognize this is war, and the battle is evidence that something in you is changing. The Holy Spirit is alive in you. And the Spirit wars against the flesh.

Romans 8:5–6 makes it clear: *"For those who live according to the flesh set their minds on the things of the flesh, but those who live according to the Spirit set their minds on the things of the Spirit. For to set the mind on the flesh is death, but to set the mind on the Spirit is life and peace."*

What you set your mind on will determine the direction of your life. In my time under the ministry of G. David Trammell, countless times he told me, "Your attitude determines your altitude." We cannot afford to be passive in our thought lives. You and I just can't afford to let anything sit in our mind rent-free. Every thought must be brought to the feet of Jesus. Every one.

Paul writes in 2 Corinthians 10:5, *"We destroy arguments and every lofty opinion raised against the knowledge of God, and* **take every thought captive to obey Christ."**

That means you take that *"I'm a failure"* thought and say: *"That doesn't align with the Word. I am a new creation in Christ."* (2 Corinthians 5:17)

You take that *"No one really cares about me"* lie and say: *"Jesus bore my rejection. He places the lonely in families."* (Psalm 68:6)

You take that *"I might as well give up"* moment and say: *"He who began a good work in me will carry it to completion."* (Philippians 1:6)

Understand this is not a chapter on self-help, it's a chapter on spiritual war. Are you saved, but stuck? Ensure you're fighting the right battle.

You can't always control what thoughts knock at your door, but you can choose which ones get to stay. Your mind is the Christian's first battlefield. And when you abide in Christ, you are not defenseless in fighting.

Distraction Is a Strategy

Many folks think they're doing well because they're not committing the "big sins," but in reality, satan doesn't need you to sin wildly. He just needs you to be too busy, too bitter, too tired, too wounded, or too carnally-minded to be spiritually aware.

The dangerous part is that not all distractions come with horns and pitchforks. Some look like endless scrolling. Some feel like overcommitment. Some sound like noble busyness. Some even feel like self-care, or the lack thereof. Distraction may not always be demonic in appearance, but it is always strategic in execution.

There are two kinds of distraction: self-distraction and enemy-distraction.

Self distraction is what we reach for when we don't want to feel. It's when we numb out to Netflix, keep our calendars full, avoid prayer time, or obsess over minor tasks to keep from dealing with deeper pain. It's when you'd rather scroll through someone else's highlight reel than sit quietly with your own soul. It's when you'd rather rage-clean the house than confront your bitterness in order to extend forgiveness. When you'd rather binge a series than ask God to search your heart. It's not always necessarily *evil*, but it's often *evasive*. Self-distraction pulls you away from your own healing.

Enemy-distraction, on the other hand, is when the enemy plants something like a thought, a situation, a conflict to reroute your attention from where God is trying to lead you. It's that oddly-timed offense right before you thought a breakthrough was coming. It's the drama that erupts the night before you planned a spiritual step forward. It's the inner narrative that ramps up just as you start to gain momentum: *"This isn't working. You're failing. Just stop. It's not worth it. It never is."*

Both types of distraction have the same result: you stop hearing, stop growing, stop building, and stop obeying. You stop being sensitive, spiritual things feel like chores, you view your pastor or your church through cloudy lenses.

Peter says, *"Be sober-minded and watchful. Your adversary the devil prowls like a roaring lion, seeking whom he may devour."* Similarly James writes,

"Submit yourselves therefore to God. Resist the devil, and he will flee from you."

Applying this scripture to our lives, we understand that we won't resist what we're not awake to. The enemy will make you think you're fighting your spouse when you're really fighting your own pride. He'll make you think your war is with your church when it's really an offense you are hanging onto (*and many times have not sought reconciliation for—see Matthew 18:15-17*) that's gone unhealed. He'll make you believe your exhaustion is physical when it's actually spiritual depletion.

So check your focus: Are you fighting symptoms or strongholds? Are you focused on what's loud or on what's lasting? Are you reacting or resisting? Stay sober and stay watchful, because distraction isn't just annoying, it's a strategy to disarm your discernment.

Put On the Armor

I love that Paul doesn't just tell us we're in a battle, but he tells us what to wear for it:

> *The belt of truth*
> *The breastplate of righteousness*

The gospel of peace on your feet
The shield of faith
The helmet of salvation
The sword of the Spirit (the Word of God)

At first, I thought Paul's words about armor were just poetic language. But the longer I've walked with God, the more I've realized this armor isn't just nice Christian language—it's essential.

See, Truth keeps me from believing lies I hear from others or from myself. Righteousness guards my heart from guilt and compromise. Peace keeps me grounded when chaos rages. Faith protects me from the flaming darts of discouragement. Salvation guards my mind when the enemy attacks my identity. The Word gives me offense. Friend, I don't just want to "make it through," I want to strike back. Do you? I've also matured enough to understand that armor doesn't put itself on. We have to choose it daily, and that's where many of us miss it. We get up, check our phones, scroll the feed, check the weather, handle an email or twelve, and rush out the door completely unarmored. Then we wonder why everything feels like it's hitting us harder than it should. We wonder why we feel stuck even though we're saved.

Armor isn't automatic. It's intentional. Putting on Truth means confronting the lies first thing in the morning. Putting on Righteousness means repenting and receiving forgiveness instead of wallowing in shame. Putting on Peace means praying proactively, before the chaos, not just reacting after it hits. Putting on Faith means choosing to believe what God said even when our circumstances haven't changed. Putting on Salvation means reminding our minds: "*I am His. I am new. I am covered.*" Putting on the Word means not just reading a verse, but absorbing it in order to wield it when the enemy shows up. I want to be quick to retaliate against the enemy with the Sword as Peter was when he sliced the Roman's ear clean off when they came to arrest Jesus. As a Christian, we have to make a daily decision to be dressed for what you cannot always see. The devil isn't waiting for you to get ready or to feel strong. He's not patiently waiting for someone to challenge him like Goliath did on the battle field. Instead, he's hoping you never will, and if I'm honest, there was a time when I was so inconsistent he didn't even have to double-check if I was challenging him. I never was. So every day, whether you feel like it or not, Friend, armor up. Not out of fear, but out of wisdom. Not to prove your strength, but to access His. Not to avoid battle, but to win it.

What to Do Now

1. Start Armed, Not Anxious
Before checking texts or social media, put on your armor through prayer: "Lord, I choose Your truth, Your righteousness, Your peace. Strengthen my faith. Guard my mind. Fill me with Your Word."

2. Identify the Real Battle
Where have you been fighting people or yourself when it's really a spiritual battle? Ask God to reveal the stronghold beneath the surface.

3. Guard Your Thought Life
Capture rogue thoughts. Journal them. Replace them with truth. Post Scripture where your eyes go most.

4. Watch Your Emotional Triggers
When you get angry, anxious, offended, or insecure, pause. What lie or wound is being touched?

5. Read the Word Like It's Your Weapon
Don't read for head knowledge. Read to resist. Read to reclaim ground. Read out loud. Use it to take back territory.

Before You Turn The Page
This isn't about becoming a better version of you. It's about waking up to the war for your soul and fighting it the right way. You're not weak, you're not helpless, you're equipped. So armor up, and fight like someone who's already been promised victory.

Reflection Questions

What have you been misdiagnosing as a natural issue when it may be spiritual?

What thoughts have gone unchallenged in your mind?

Which piece of the armor have you been neglecting?

What truth from Scripture do you need to start speaking daily?

Where do you need to shift from defense to offense?

Scriptures to Read and Meditate On
Ephesians 6:10–18
2 Corinthians 10:3–5
Romans 8:5–6
1 Peter 5:8–10
Isaiah 54:17
James 4:7
Colossians 2:13–15

Prayer
Lord, open my eyes to the real war. Teach me to see through the noise and distraction. Help me recognize the enemy's schemes and resist with authority. I choose Your armor today. Strengthen my spirit, sharpen my focus, and fill me with boldness. Remind me that I don't fight for victory—I fight from victory. In Jesus' name, Amen.

Chapter Five
The Power of Confession
James 5:16, 1 John 1:5–9,
Psalm 32:1–5, Proverbs 28:13

There comes a point in your journey where a situational breakthrough won't come from another sermon, another fast, another altar call, another church service, or another journal entry. It will only come when you open your mouth and say the words you've been terrified to say: *"I'm stuck. I messed up. I need help."*

I laughed when I typed those words because I know it's not that easy. True confession is one of the most difficult spiritual acts we're called to do because of how brutally humbling it is. It forces us to let someone else see what you've tried and failed to manage privately. That's terrifying! I had to confess one time to my Pastor that I had been watching pornography. It was terrifying, and to be honest, it was one of the most embarrassing things I've ever admitted. But that conversation cracked the door to healing.

We struggle with confession because we wonder if

our confession will change how they see us. What if our reputation suffers? We wouldn't want that in our Church circles. Of course, our confession might even confirm our own worst fear, that maybe we really are broken. Due to the "hide it" culture many churches have intentionally or unintentionally created or propagated, confession sometimes feels more sinful than the sin itself.

If we're truthful, sometimes say we believe in grace while we're still trying to earn belonging. So we hide our struggle and polish our image. We learn to smile and say, *"I'm blessed,"* or, *"God is good!"* even though we're bleeding out.

While churches should be the safest place to confess, for some, they've become the scariest because we've seen people judged, shamed, sidelined, or gossiped about the moment they got honest. There is an unspoken culture in churches where we praise the polish and not the progress. They value standards of language, dress, or interaction more than they value internal growth, intentional progress, or interpersonal development.

That shouldn't be the case.

While there is much value in standards of dress and conduct, the Body of Christ should stop striving to be an art gallery full of polished pieces and get back to the roots of it's purpose: to be safe house for sinners in recovery, a home for the prodigal, and a hospital for the broken. We say we know this, but yet, many walk into church wearing invisible armor because they're not sure His people can handle their truth.

Some church folk have made heroes out of hiding and confused anointing with invincibility. Worse, they pretend that deliverance means folks no longer struggle. This "art gallery mentality" turns into the air the church breathes. So when someone admits they still wrestle, we don't know what to do with them. Therefore, they become *the other.*

But here's the truth: confession is not weakness. It's a weapon in warfare. If we're not confessing our sin, if we're not repenting, then we are not fighting as effectively and efficiently as possible. Of course we need to practice care in regard to whom and how we confess; we shouldn't tie a big sign around our neck that says, "I stole batteries at Walmart" and walk into church. Yet, we should prioritize confession all the same. It takes courage to say, *"I'm not okay."*

It takes maturity to say, *"I need help."* It takes faith to believe that healing is worth the risk of being seen. Some of the biggest faith-walkers I know have had moments of vulnerability where they have openly said, *"I messed that up."*

There is beauty in scripture we don't let ourselves see: our Bibles do not shame confession. Instead, they honor it. Your Bible says confession is the doorway to healing, not humiliation. James 5:16, *"Therefore, **confess** your sins to one another and pray for one another, **that you may be healed**."*

Healthy confession isn't about exposing you, but it's about liberating you. I admit this is why you have to be careful with how and who you confess to, but the necessity of carefulness doesn't mean we shouldn't confess at all. Do the hard thing, even though it's hard. What stays in the dark will always have power over you, but what comes into the light begins to lose its grip. This is the liberating power of confession!

Healthy confession is not performance-driven, it's not oversharing, and it's doesn't live for attention. It doesn't blurt things out because you were caught. It is holy and healing—the kind that cracks the door to the dark room and lets light flood in.

Further Dissecting the Cycle

The Saved But Stuck Cycle doesn't just revolve around sin as many believe. It revolves around silence. This is how I see it:

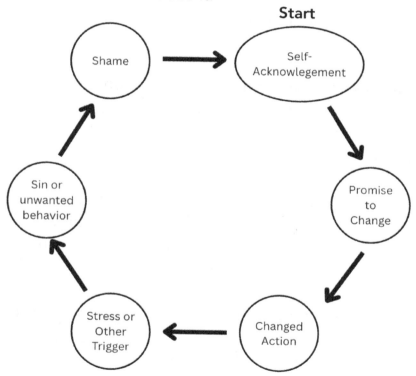

As long as you stay silent, the enemy has leverage. He knows you'll keep pretending. He knows you'll keep isolating. He knows you'll sit in the same pew every week, raising your hands while sinking in shame. Why does this work so well? Friend, the enemy of our soul understands and believes what many believers don't: confession breaks the cycle.

While forgiveness comes directly from God, healing often comes through His Body. The moment you speak it out loud to another believer, three things happen:

The silence is broken: Shame's grip loosens immediately because it only thrives in silence and secrecy. When you name it out loud, you take authority back.

The fear shrinks: What felt massive in the dark becomes manageable in the light. It's no longer some unbeatable monster. Now it's *Only a Flesh Wound*, and wounds can be healed.

Accountability is born: You're no longer carrying it alone. You're walking with someone who can check in, speak life, and hold space for your process.

This is why the enemy works so hard to convince you to stay quiet and keep it to yourself. He doesn't even care if you feel holy conviction, as long as you stay silent. He knows that a confessing believer is a dangerous believer because once you confess, you no longer believe the illusion that isolation is safer.

But let's name the elephant in the room: What if you confess, and they judge you? What if the person you choose talks behind your back? What if your reputation takes a hit? I'm not naive to that. I've seen people open up and get mishandled. I've seen leaders respond with legalism instead of grace. I've seen Christians weaponize information instead of steward it. And yes, I've seen Christians gossip about others in the name of *"praying for them."*

Yes, it's a risk. But here's what I believe with everything in me: the risk of staying silent is far more dangerous than the risk of being judged.

Friend, what you don't confess, you carry alone, and what you carry alone will eventually crush you. I want more for you than that. God wants more for you than that.

No, you don't confess to everyone. But you must confess to someone. Someone trustworthy and grace-filled. Someone mature enough to cover you, pray with you, and walk alongside you.

If you don't have that person yet, earnestly ask God to send them. I really struggled with finding my person. More than a couple well-meaning men promised me things and fell short, forgetting they made commitments to me. I wanted to give up, but I kept praying. Finally, God sent me someone, but I pulled a Gideon. I laid out fleeces. I needed to know God had truly sent this person. Part of me felt bad, but I wanted to make sure he was committed and that he was safe. And he was, and still is.

I've seen God do the same thing for others, too. And if He's done it before, He will do it again. I believe He wants to. He never designed you to walk this out alone. So if you want the cycle to break, your silence must break first. Confession is not about making a show of yourself, or begging, or embarrassing yourself to prove your repentance. It's about stepping out of the darkness into the light and finally letting your soul breathe again.

Let me speak to your heart: you are not disqualified and you are not too messy. You are not too far gone. Confession might just be the doorway into the very healing you've been praying for all along.

How to Confess Well

Confession is holy, but it's also vulnerable, and it matters how and to whom you confess.

1. Go to God First

Always start with Him. Not as a ritual, but as a return. Come clean before the One who already knows. Say it raw. Say it plainly. No hiding.

2. Choose Safe People

Don't confess to just anyone. Confess to someone who is spiritually mature, compassionate, and committed to truth. A pastor. A mentor. A godly friend. Someone who won't excuse sin, but also won't weaponize your vulnerability.

3. Be Specific, Not Self-Loathing

You don't need to spiral. You don't need to relive every detail. Just be clear about what you did, why you're bringing it into the light, and what kind of support you need.

4. Receive Grace Without Delay

Don't confess and then reject forgiveness. Confession is not a performance to earn mercy, it's an open door to receive it.

5. Walk in the Light Going Forward

Confession isn't the end, but the beginning. Start building a life of honesty. Normalize light. Stay in community. Keep short accounts. Let your daily walk be marked by honesty, not hiding.

This is what it looks like when you swap out silence for confession:

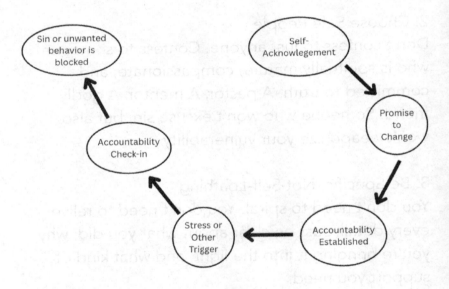

The Cycle is broken! Notice there are new accountability steps—maybe for you this would mean: Confessing your porn addiction (confession), making a covenant with God in prayer to resist (promise), installing Covenant Eyes on your cell phone (establish) and linking up with a buddy to monitor your activity regularly (check-in). Knowing that your buddy will get a notification if you slip keeps you honest and pure, away from that sin.

Or maybe it's finally prioritizing God—you confess you have not been reading the Word. You make a covenant with God about this, and commit to a daily or weekly Bible reading plan (establish). You send a bi-weekly recap to your pastor (check-in), and knowing that you have to send a "report" holds you to your promise.

Whatever you need help with, accountability is the ultimate cheat code for success.

Pro Tip: If you are someone's accountability partner, remember, accountability feels like an attack when they're not used to it. Hold people accountable with grace.

What to Do Now

1. Confess it to God first. Say it plainly. No fancy words. No hiding.

2. Say it out loud. Name what you've buried. Let your voice break the silence.

3. Tell one safe person. Ask for prayer. Ask for help. Set a time and stick to it.

4. Establish check-in rhythm. Weekly, monthly—whatever works. But don't disappear again.

5. Fight shame with Scripture. Replace that cycle of guilt with truth. Start with Psalm 32 and 1 John 1.

Before You Turn The Page

If you're thinking *"I can't say this out loud,"* that's exactly what needs to be said. You don't need to bleed quietly. You don't need to fake strength. You've bled long enough in silence. You've faked strength just to survive. Now, it's time to be seen.

Reflection Questions

What's the hardest part about confession for you?

Where in your life have you chosen silence over honesty?

Who is a safe person you can invite into your healing?

What lie has shame made you believe?

How might your life look different if you lived fully in the light?

Scriptures to Read and Meditate On
James 5:16
1 John 1:5–9
Psalm 32:1–5
Proverbs 28:13
John 8:12
Hebrews 4:13–16

Prayer
Father, I confess what I've been carrying. I've hidden, I've minimized, I've justified—but I don't want to stay in the dark anymore. Shine Your light into the places I've sealed off. Search me. Cleanse me. Heal me. I trust You with the truth. I trust You with my healing. I choose honesty. I choose freedom. I choose light. In Jesus' name, Amen.

Chapter Six
Don't Waste the Wilderness
Exodus 13:17–22, Deuteronomy 8:2–3,
Luke 4:1–14, Isaiah 43:19

Everyone wants to get out of their wilderness season, when they feel alone or lost. We see these times as punishment or abandonment, but what if God led you into the wilderness as preparation? I know, My Friend, it sounds like a cliche and you might even be rolling your eyes. Stay with me. What if it's true, that the only place God can meet you as you are is in the wilderness?

We don't preach, teach, or talk about the wilderness often because it's not glamorous, fast, or victorious. Our wilderness doesn't get us subscribers, followers, or donors. Seasons of wilderness are dry, lonely, and quiet. They mess with your head. In many cases, they last far longer than we think they should.

But if you're going to get unstuck, you are going to have to learn how to continuously walk forward through seasons when nothing seems to be working, when prayers echo back in silence, and when clarity feels out of reach. You have to learn how to push ahead even when God seems out of sight. Walk through your wilderness like it's holy ground—because it is.

Why the Wilderness Matters

I hate wilderness moments, let alone seasons of it. It's difficult, brutal, disorienting, lonely, and long. Not to mention, I've never walked into a wilderness season and been handed a map, compass, or rescue date to circle on my calendar.

Most wilderness days feel like losses. We lose clarity, confidence, and peace. We lose people we thought would stay, or at least help. People who say we can reach out when we need it—only to be met with silence or "competing priorities" when we finally do.

The wilderness breaks your routine. It messes with your sense of control, and will strip away the comforts you didn't realize you depended on. And yes, it will confront everything in you that still expects your faith to work like a vending machine: insert prayer, receive breakthrough.

Some days it feels like you're grieving something, but you can't quite name what. You miss how things used to feel. You miss what your walk with God used to look like. You wonder if you did something wrong. You start doubting if He's still with you. You question everything, and yet, it's in this barren, uncomfortable, unrelenting season that God does some of His deepest work.

When God led Israel out of Egypt, He didn't take them the fastest way to the Promised Land. Exodus 13 says He took them the long way around through the wilderness because they weren't ready for battle. In other words, the shortcut would have killed them—or at least, broke them.

Friend, God knew what they didn't. There was more to the physical walk out of Egypt. They had to unlearn some spiritual things. They had been slaves for generations. Slavery had gotten into their bones. Into their speech. Into their sense of identity. Into how they related to authority. Into how they prayed and trusted and thought about the future.

They didn't just need freedom from Pharaoh, they needed freedom from themselves. So God led them into the wilderness to prepare them. Deuteronomy 8:2–3 says it clearly: *"Remember the whole way that the Lord your God has led you these forty years in the wilderness, that he might humble you, testing you to know what was in your heart, whether you would keep his commandments or not. And he humbled you and let you hunger and fed you with manna, which you did not know, nor did your fathers know, that he might make you know that man does not live by bread alone, but man lives by every word that comes from the mouth of the Lord."*

God can teach you more while you're alone in the wilderness than success can teach you in front of others. Wilderness seasons slow us down, humble us, and reveal our real priorities.

It's in the wilderness that you learn that prayer isn't a religious activity or ritual, it's like air to the spiritual man. In the wilderness you learn that worship isn't about a song, let alone if the song is *"old enough," "new enough,"* or performed at the loudness or at the tempo that we prefer. Worship is about surrender. It's in the wilderness that you learn how God's Word isn't an optional book on your shelf available for your professional development or self-help when you need it. His Word becomes your bread. Most importantly, it's in the wilderness that we learn how God is not just our escape plan, but how He is our sustainer and our very source of life.

The wilderness taught me not to just cry out to Him in trouble, but how to cling to Him in dryness. How to follow even when I can't feel Him. How to trust even when it doesn't make sense. How to listen for the whisper, not just for the thunder. God is still speaking to His people like He did to Elijah in 1 Kings 19:12—the *low whisper.* Can you hear it?

If not, let the wilderness do what it is meant to do: detox your ears.

We would do well to embrace the wilderness as it clears out the noise, cuts through the clutter, removes our idols and burns off our pride. Let it break your addiction to being seen. Let it empty the parts of you that still crave applause to feel like you matter.

Friend, the wilderness hurts. But it also heals. It strips, but it also rebuilds. It tests, but it also strengthens. You don't have to come out of the wilderness the same or worse. You don't have to come out bitter, hardened, and still stuck in Egypt in your mind. You have the ability to come out formed by fire, rooted in truth, and ready to walk in the kind of freedom that lasts.

The wilderness matters because it's where God rewrites the story you tell yourself. It's where He rebuilds your identity. It's where He's building the strength in you to carry the calling that would have crushed you if it came too soon. Don't waste it.

Jesus Went There Too

You are not alone in your wilderness experience. Luke 3-4 tells us that Jesus himself went into the wilderness after being baptized. Get this: as he prayed and was baptized, the heavens opened as a voice declared, "You are my beloved Son; with you I am well pleased." Pretty impressive, especially seeing that it's in this moment His wilderness began. What I want you to understand, Friend, is that the wilderness wasn't a result of disobedience and it wasn't punishment. It was part of the process He had to go through. Jesus didn't wander into the wilderness. He was led there.

He went with power and in weakness. He fasted and was still tempted. The enemy came with suggestion after suggestion, just like he does with us:

To Jesus: *"Turn these stones into bread."*

To us: *"Take matters into your own hands. You can fix this yourself. Just do what feels good right now."*

To Jesus: *"Throw yourself down; God will protect you."*

To us: *"Make a reckless choice. If God really loves you, He'll bail you out anyway."*

To Jesus: *"Bow to me and I'll give you everything you see."*

To us: *"Compromise your integrity. Take the shortcut. You can have success, recognition, and influence without God."*

The temptation wasn't just about food or power, but it was about identity. It was about shortcutting the plan and trading the eternal for the immediate. But Jesus didn't bend. He didn't try to debate the devil with feelings or reasoning. He didn't try to perform His way through it. He answered each lie with the Word:

"It is written."

Every time He said it, something broke in the spiritual realm. Do you see it? The wilderness didn't take His power away, but it revealed how anchored He was in Truth.

Let's make this real: if God in flesh walked into the wilderness on purpose, with no shortcut, no applause, no quick fix... why do we think we should be exempt? Why do we deserve a *"Get Out of the Wilderness Free"* card?

If Jesus, our perfect example, endured temptation, isolation, and spiritual resistance for forty days before stepping into public ministry, what makes us think we can skip that process? Jesus wasn't being punished, He was being proven. So are we.

When He came out of the wilderness, Luke 4:14 says He returned *"in the power of the Spirit."*

That's what God wants for you too—to exit the wilderness in the power of His Spirit. God isn't leading you into dry seasons so you die there, but to go through them and come out with a power that you didn't have before. A maturity that can carry the weight of what's coming, and a Word deep enough to stand on when everything else shakes.

The wilderness didn't disqualify Jesus, it launched Him. And it will do the same for you, if you don't run from it.

Signs You're in a Wilderness Season

What's tricky is that you don't always know you're in the wilderness when it begins. It doesn't come with a flashing warning sign, but starts subtly. You begin to feel dry, even while doing all the right things. You're still praying, still showing up to church, still reading your Bible, but nothing seems to stir your spirit the way used to. Worship feels like motion. The Word feels distant. You wonder if something's wrong with you.

You look around and realize people who once walked closely with you have fallen away, or worse, they're still present but disconnected. Relationships shift. Loneliness creeps in. You start to question your place. There's a dull ache that follows you into your quiet time. A feeling that your prayers aren't hitting the ceiling or they're getting lost somewhere on the way up. Even though you know God is still good, you don't feel Him as near.

You're not tempted to run away from God, but you also don't feel on fire for Him. You're not in outright rebellion, but you're not thriving either. You're just... surviving. You're not moved by the things that used to stir you. The stuff that once gave you energy now feels heavy. You're checking all the boxes, but something's off. The smile stays fixed while your soul quietly aches. Outwardly stable, inwardly unraveling. But then you begin noticing patterns reappearing like old fears, old mindsets, old temptations and you're asking yourself, *"What? Why now? Why me? Why this again?"* There's a heaviness you can't explain.

If that's where you are, Friend, you're not broken. **You're in the wilderness.** We can be okay with this, because it means God can do something beneath the surface that's more important than what's happening above it—if we let Him.

What Not to Do in the Wilderness

Don't rush your wilderness. You can't microwave maturity, and if God is doing something in you, trying to skip it will just delay your development.

Don't numb your wilderness. Avoiding the pain with distractions won't make it go away. Wilderness seasons are invitations to presence. So sit with God, even when He feels silent.

Don't isolate in your wilderness. Yes, it feels lonely, but you were not made to go through it alone. Find others who can walk with you, pray with you, and remind you of truth.

Don't interpret silence as absence. Remember that sometimes, the teacher is quiet during the test.

What to Do Now

1. Be Honest With God
Tell Him how it feels. He already knows. Honesty is worship.

2. Feed on the Word
You won't survive this season without Scripture. Write it. Read it. Speak it. Stand on it.

3. Anchor Your Identity
The enemy will lie. Loudly. Remind yourself daily of who you are in Christ.

4. Watch for Provision
God sent manna. God sent angels. He's sending what you need. Look for it.

5. Lean Into the Process
Don't flinch from the fire. Ask God what He's forging in you. Let Him chisel what doesn't belong. Yield to the shaping. Trust that it isn't random, but strategically surgical.

Before You Turn The Page

The wilderness is not wasted. It is where the shallow dies and the sacred is refined. It's where your appetites shift. Where your strength is tested. Where your roots grow deep. It is not where God abandons you but where He remakes you.

I know the ache of it. I've walked through the kind of spiritual dryness where even worship felt hollow and prayer was work. But I've also seen what God does in the silence. I've learned He speaks loudest when the noise dies down. So don't quit here. Don't numb out. Don't camp in what was meant to be a passage. Keep walking. Not just to get out, but to come out changed. Because when this wilderness ends, and it will, you'll carry something forged in the fire. And that kind of freedom can't be shaken.

Reflection Questions

1. When God feels distant, what's your first reaction, and what does that reveal about your relationship with Him?

2. What has this wilderness season uncovered about your view of yourself, your worth, or your faith?

3. Where have you been numbing instead of kneeling? Escaping instead of enduring?

4. Have there been signs of God's provision in this season that you've overlooked or dismissed?

5. If God is preparing you through this, what kind of person do you believe He's shaping you to become?

Scriptures to Read and Meditate On
Exodus 13:17–22
Deuteronomy 8:2–3
Luke 4:1–14
Isaiah 43:19
Psalm 63
Romans 5:3–5
Hebrews 12:11

Prayer
*God, I don't always understand what You're doing.
This season feels dry. Lonely. Heavy. But I trust that
You're leading me. Help me not to waste this
wilderness. Teach me to lean on You. To feed on
Your Word. To surrender to the process. Let this
place become an altar, not a prison. Remind me of
who I am, and show me what You're growing in me
through this. In Jesus' name, Amen.*

Chapter Seven
Learning to Live Free
Galatians 5:1, Romans 6:11–14,
John 15:1–8, Philippians 2:12–13

Getting free is one thing but living free is another. Many people have a breakthrough moment during a service, a prayer, or a moment of clarity where they realize, *"I don't have to live bound anymore."* They take that first step into freedom with tears streaming down their face, hands lifted, hope rising.

Monday doesn't come with music and tears. It comes with dishes in the sink, bills on the counter, and thoughts you thought you'd left behind. You wake up with the memory of Sunday's freedom, but the weight of Tuesday's struggle. The enemy whispers again, and the habits resurface. Before long, they start wondering, *"Was I ever really free to begin with?"*

That struggle is where this chapter comes in, because freedom isn't just something God does for you, it's something He teaches you to walk in.

Freedom Is a Daily Decision

Galatians 5:1 says, *"For freedom Christ has set us free; stand firm therefore, and do not submit again to a yoke of slavery."* Notice the language: Christ already set us free but we still have to stand firm in that freedom. It's like holding a winning lottery ticket. Freedom was yours the moment Jesus said it was finished, but living in it means showing up and claiming it every day.

It's a thousand small choices, one after another:

> *Choosing truth over lies.*
> *Choosing light over hiding.*
> *Choosing community over isolation.*
> *Choosing Scripture over spiraling thoughts.*
> *Choosing surrender over self-will.*

Romans 6:11–14 puts it this way: *"consider yourselves dead to sin and alive to God in Christ Jesus... let not sin therefore reign... Do not present your members to sin as instruments for unrighteousness, but present yourselves to God..."*

It's important to call out the language here is active, not passive, because we can't just comfortably float into freedom. We must walk into it, one foot in front of the other, and take it one day at a time.

What Living Free Looks Like
Living free doesn't mean you never struggle and it certainly doesn't mean you never get tempted. It means you don't go back to chains when the door is open. It means you stop normalizing what God died to deliver you from. It means when temptation comes, you don't just try harder to resist, but you lean into grace more quickly. It means when fear creeps in, you don't hide, but you confess and get prayer. Call it what it is: That *"just one more time"* is a trap. That *"this is just how I cope"* is a lie. The moment you name it, you take the first step toward walking out of it.

Living free means:

> *You catch lies faster.*
> *You repent quicker.*
> *You recover stronger.*
> *You stay rooted longer.*

Remember, Friend, this walk we walk is not about perfection, but about progress. It's about persistence. It's about getting up and trying again when you have a thousand reasons not to. It's standing up even if it takes all the strength you have. It's about putting one foot in front of the other, even if it's only a fraction of an inch. I'm here for you, and I'll celebrate with you any small progress. Walking in freedom doesn't mean you stop fighting, it means you finally know how to fight—and fight you do.

Your Fruit Is the Evidence

A while back, I visited a friend's home and noticed a beautiful bowl of fruit on the kitchen table. Shiny apples, bright oranges, even a bunch of grapes draped perfectly across the side. It looked perfect. But when I reached out and grabbed an apple, I realized it wasn't real. It was plastic! Glossy and hollow, completely inedible.

Friend, that's how some of us have lived. Beautifully arranged, socially acceptable, spiritually presentable... but hollow inside. You can only keep up appearances for so long. Because when life takes a bite out of you—and it will—you'll either bruise like something real or crack like something fake. Real fruit might not be flawless, but it nourishes. It's alive. It multiplies. It has weight. Fake fruit? It just looks the part.

Don't settle for a bowl of performance. Stay connected to the Vine and let God grow something real.

Jesus said in John 15:5, *"If you remain in Me, and I in you, you **will** bear much fruit."*

The proof that you're living free isn't just in how loud you shout, how long you pray, how passionately you worship, or how long you can fast. The proof isn't how polished you are on Sundays and Wednesdays at church. You can rehearse church culture all you want and still be rotting inside. Eventually, it will show. But real fruit doesn't wilt in pressure, it nourishes.

It's the Love that reaches even when it's hard, the Joy that shows up in hardship, the Peace that quiets the noise, the Patience that slows your reactions, and the Self-Control that holds the line.

Fruit doesn't come from trying harder, but from staying connected to The Vine. John 15 is clear: the branch doesn't produce fruit on its own. It produces by abiding in the vine.

Friend, this is your job now! Not to perform or to prove, but to abide.

Your Freedom Has a Purpose

You weren't set free just to feel better, or to stop sinning, or so you could sit quietly in a pew, hoping nobody asks too many questions about your past. You were set free so you could live. Really live. Free to breathe without guilt hanging over your shoulders. Free to stand in a room and know that you belong there. Free to love without fear of being exposed. Free to serve without ever having to hear that haunting whisper, *"Who do you think you are?"*

God rescues you to restore your identity. There's a calling on your life. A purpose. A mission. And that thing you thought disqualified you? That very place of bondage, that cycle you were stuck in, that wilderness you've walked through? God will use that story to unlock freedom in someone else.

Your pain will preach. Your healing will point people home. Your freedom will break generational curses not just off you, but off your family.

Don't sit down in shame when God is calling you to stand up in boldness. Don't silence your voice when

God is ready to amplify your testimony. Don't let fear convince you that you're not ready.

You don't have to be perfect to be purposeful. You just have to be free. While there will be days you feel unqualified, and there will be moments when you hear the enemy whisper, *"You're still the same person,"* but that's when you stand in the mirror and declare what God says about you: *"I am a new creation. I am redeemed. I am called. I am walking in purpose on purpose."*

That's just it, Friend: Living in freedom means walking in purpose on purpose.

You didn't come this far just to make it out. You came out to go back and help someone else. You came out to build something, to lead something, to love boldly, to live fully, to serve joyfully… to shine where you used to shrink. Your freedom is not the end of the story. It's the start of your ministry.

What to Do Now

1. Name One Chain You Refuse to Wear Again
Write it down, and call it what it is. Say out loud:
"I'm not going back to this."

2. Build a Rhythm That Keeps You Rooted:
Word, worship, community.

3. Share Your Story With Someone Else.
Text, call, or message one person this week. Say,
"God brought me out, and He can do it for you
too."

3. Preach to Yourself
Memorize Galatians 5:1 and speak it daily: "Christ
has set me free. I will not go back."

5. Stay Connected, Not Just Committed
Don't just do the work—stay in the presence. Abide.
Breathe. Don't just resist... rest in Him

Before You Turn The Page
The same God who broke your chains is the God
who will teach you how to walk without them.
Freedom isn't a one-time miracle, it's a lifestyle.
Each and every day, you get to choose it again.

Reflection Questions

What does freedom mean to you right now?

Where do you still act like you're bound, even though you've been set free?

What habits help you stay rooted in Christ?

Who needs to hear your story of freedom?

What's going to change now?

Scriptures to Read and Meditate On
Galatians 5:1
Romans 6:11–14
John 15:1–8
Philippians 2:12–13
2 Corinthians 3:17
Colossians 2:6–7

Prayer
Lord, thank You for setting me free. Now teach me how to live like it. Remind me every day that I don't have to go back to who I was. Help me to stay rooted in Your truth, in Your love, in Your grace. Make me sensitive to the small steps that either pull me back or push me forward. Let my life bear fruit that points to You. And let my freedom be a light for others who still feel stuck. In Jesus' name, Amen.

Conclusion
Our Table Talk

You've come a long way, and I'm proud of you.

Through this book, we've smiled, laughed, and cried together. We've reflected, prayed, and made some real changes. We confessed and we decided to embrace the wilderness.

Friend, you've fought battles nobody knows about, and yet, you kept turning the page.

The fact that you're still here tells me something loud and clear: you don't want a surface fix. You want freedom, and no longer just the temporary kind. Not the Instagram kind. Not the church-face-on-Sunday kind. You want the kind of freedom that gets down in your bones, the kind that doesn't wash off in a bad week. The kind that rebuilds everything the enemy tried to destroy.

If I could sit across the table from you right now, no microphone, no pulpit, just me and you, I would look you in the eyes, and tell you the truth your soul has been aching to believe:

My Friend, You are not too far gone. You are not too much. You are not too late. You are not stuck forever.

My Dear Friend, I don't care how many relapses you've had. I don't care how long it's been since you felt close to God. I don't care what the religious people said about you. You are not beyond the reach of grace. You are not disqualified from deliverance.

Believe me: You are not forgotten by your Father.

Maybe you've gone from altar call to altar call, from late-night sob sessions to morning guilt spirals. Maybe you've tried to numb it, outrun it, spiritualize it. Maybe you've screamed into your pillow wondering, *"Why am I still here? Why can't I change?"*

And maybe now, you're scared to believe again. Because what if it doesn't work this time either? Let me tell you the truth: Fear is not your future, shame is not your name, and heaviness is not your inheritance.

The God who raised the dead isn't intimidated by your dysfunction. The God who spoke galaxies into existence isn't frustrated by your process. The God who wrapped Himself in flesh and took on your sin is not surprised by your struggle.

He's still here, calling, pursuing, and fighting for the real you under all the coping mechanisms. Even when you don't feel free, He's still working.

You didn't stumble into this book, Friend. This wasn't random. You didn't "happen" to pick it up during a low week. This was divine. The Spirit of the Living God orchestrated this moment because He refuses to leave you where you are.

The chains you've carried? They're not welded shut. The lies you believed? They can be broken. The guilt you've carried? It's already been nailed to the cross.

So what now?

If you've fallen, get up. If you've failed, come clean. If you've been faking it, take the mask off.

Freedom is not a one-time altar moment. It's not a good song on Sunday or a highlight reel of good behavior. Freedom is the Person of Jesus Christ, meeting you right here, in the middle of your unfinished mess, and saying: Let's walk this out together.

This same Jesus who met the woman caught in adultery—surrounded by stones and shame—and said, *"Neither do I condemn you. Go and sin no more."* This same Jesus who told the man stuck on a mat, *"Get up. Pick up what's been carrying you. Walk."* This same Jesus who made breakfast for the one who denied Him.

He is the same Jesus stepping into your story right now. Not with shame or anger, but with eyes full of compassion. With hands still scarred but stretched out toward you. And Friend, there are tears in my own eyes as I tell you how He's saying: *I still want you. I still choose you. I'm still here.*

You may feel tired, but you're not finished. You may feel weak, but His power is made perfect in weakness. You may feel disqualified, but God delights in using the ones who thought they'd never be used again.

So let me plead with you, like a friend, like a brother, like a pastor, like someone who's been stuck and has seen the light:

Don't settle. Don't go back. Don't pretend you're fine when you know there's more. Don't waste another year of your life decorating a prison cell Jesus already unlocked.

Lift your head. Square your shoulders. Speak to the fear, to the shame, to the cycle. Speak to the voice that told you it's too late. Then, walk. Even if your knees are shaking and your voice is trembling. Even if you don't know where the next step will lead. Walk out of Egypt. Walk out of the grave. Walk into the newness that's already been written over your name.

You are not stuck. You are not your worst day. You are not your darkest thought. You are not who they said you'd always be. You are redeemed. You are called. You are chosen. You are free. Now go live like it.

In Jesus' name, My Friend,

Amen.

Saved but Stuck
For Every Believer Who is Tired of Pretending

Epilogue
The Journey Continues

You've made it to the end of these pages, but this is not the end of your story.

You've been reminded of your identity, and you've learned how to fight the right battles. You've sat with the pain of the wilderness. You've dared to believe that confession brings healing. You've heard the call to walk in the freedom already purchased for you. But now the question becomes: What will you do with what you've received?

Freedom isn't just a gift, it's an invitation. Not just for you, but for those still living in the same chains you've been set free from. This journey isn't just about personal breakthrough, but about becoming the kind of person who helps someone else break through too.

There's someone in your world right now: at your workplace, in your friend circle, maybe even sitting next to you at church, who is silently stuck. Someone who is drowning in shame, hiding in cycles, afraid to speak up. And they don't need a sermon. They need a story. But not just any story... they need your story.

You are now a carrier of freedom. So when the time comes:

> *Speak truth, even if your voice trembles.*
>
> *Share your journey, even if it's still messy.*
>
> *Offer prayer, even when you're not sure what to say.*
>
> *Sit in silence with someone until they can find their words.*

Refuse to look away when someone opens up about what they're carrying. Your scars aren't a liability. They're a testimony. Your weakness doesn't disqualify you but it makes you approachable. Your freedom isn't the end goal. It's the beginning of your ministry.

Let the enemy regret every chain he ever tried to use against you. Let hell tremble when you walk into rooms carrying the presence of God and the wisdom of your process. Let your freedom echo into your family, your church, your community.

So when you wake up tomorrow and the weight feels familiar, don't panic. Just return to what you've learned: You're not stuck. You're walking it out. And now, you're helping someone else walk too. The journey continues, and so does your assignment. You've been called, and you've been delivered. Best of all, you've been equipped.

Go be a Friend for someone else.
You have my blessing.

With all my heart,

Your Friend,

Anthony

About the Author

Rev. Anthony Miller has a passion for helping people find real freedom in Jesus Christ. A bold communicator and unapologetically honest writer, Anthony has spent his life proclaiming that the church is not a museum for the polished, but a hospital for the hurting. His voice carries the weight of someone who's lived through it— fought the battles, wrestled with shame, stood at the edge of giving up—and kept walking anyway.

Anthony leads with conviction, compassion, and clarity, preaching the gospel in a way that reaches both the broken and the burned-out. He's committed to tearing off the masks that religion often rewards, confronting spiritual cycles that keep people stuck, and pointing readers back to the God who doesn't flinch at mess but meets us in it.

Anthony writes, publishes, and equips believers through books, resources, and coaching rooted in restoration, spiritual identity, and Kingdom impact. He serves the Body of Christ with one goal: to help people move from stuck to sent, from surviving to walking in purpose on purpose.

He is a shepherd, a builder, and a reminder that Grace still runs toward the prodigal, that Truth still breaks chains, and the Gospel still works.

Anthony has sat on many Boards of Directors, had face time with many influential people, has built connections with some of the most prominent people in various organizations, and physically cannot stop reaching for the stars of success.

But none of that matters without being able to come home and squeeze his insanely talented and beautiful wife, Danielle, and his three incredible God-honoring children, Michael, Matthew, and Marcus. While "competing priorities" is a common term for his day-to-day work, these four special people are always the first.

A.W. Tozer once said, "Refuse to be average. Let your heart soar as high as it will." If Anthony could add one thing to this favorite quote, it would be, "And in all your soaring, remember who you're soaring for—because the view means more when you share it with the ones you love."

The Reasons I Soar

Made in the USA
Monee, IL
01 July 2025

20345659R00085